Reco·mind·o

Mindful Recomendos for Life and Work

Claudia Dawson

Recomendo

All of the recommendations and mindful tips in this book were selected from Recomendo, a free weekly newsletter produced by Kevin Kelly, Mark Frauenfelder and Claudia Dawson. Each Sunday we send out a short list of 6 personal recommendations of useful and cool things. Sign up at recomendo.com to join almost 60,000 other happy subscribers. Or use this QR code.

Disclosure

In the case of a product recommendation, the QR code will often direct to an affiliate link that gives us a small referral fee. This fee helps to pay for the Recomendo site and newsletter, and the cost of producing this book. But none of my reviews have been paid for by others, or rely on free samples, or are product placements.

Copyright

For the writers and artists and content creators who share their work freely and boldly.

Thank you for igniting my imagination and inspiring me to be a better human.

Contents

Introduction

Reco•mind•o is a mindfully curated selection of my personal recommendations published in Recomendo — a weekly newsletter co-written by Kevin Kelly, Mark Frauenfelder and me.

Each Sunday, we send out an email of 6 brief recommendations of cool and useful things. Since 2016 we have shared more than 2,000 recommendations in over 300 issues, and have almost 60,000 subscribers.

Over the past several years, the way I consume media, products and ideas has changed. For myself, a cool and useful thing is something that expands my mind, enhances my life or grows my spirit.

In this book I've tried to include less physical items and more actionable advice that you can benefit from without having to buy anything. You'll find tips for mindful eating, tools for reading, ways to self-soothe, and visuals to change your perspective on productivity and happiness.

I chose past Recomendos that have been more than a cool or useful thing to me. The recommendations in this book are tools for thought and habits to adopt which have profoundly changed my way of being or seeing.

I am grateful to all the bloggers, thinkers, and content creators whose work I've shared in this book. I've tried to credit all the original creators, and in most cases you'll find the QR codes will direct you to their published work or personal websites.

Claudia Dawson
claudia@cool-tools.org
@clauddaws

Better Living

*"The most courageous decision
that you can make each day is to
be in a good mood."*

— Voltaire

List of truths

This list of David Cain's 88 important truths are all aha moments for me. Here are a few of them:

- Bad moods will come and go your whole life, and trying to force them away makes them run deeper and last longer.
- Cynicism is far too easy to be useful.
- Every problem you have is your responsibility, regardless of who caused it.
- Wishing things were different is a great way to torture yourself.

Six right livelihood guidelines

No matter your background or beliefs, these wise and compassionate Buddhist guidelines for living are simply vital. Here are the ones I am trying to adopt: Consume mindfully — Eat with awareness and gratitude. Pause before buying and see if breathing is enough. Pay attention to the effects of media you consume.

Six Right Livelihood Guidelines

1. Consume Mindfully.
Eat with awareness and gratitude.
Pause before buying and see if breathing is enough.
Pay attention to the effects of media you consume.

2. Pause. Breathe. Listen.
When you feel compelled to speak in a meeting or conversation, pause.
Breathe before entering your home, place of work, or school.
Listen to the people you encounter. They are buddhas.

3. Practice Gratitude.
Notice what you have.
Be equally grateful for opportunities and challenges.
Share joy, not negativity.

4. Cultivate Compassion and Loving Kindness.
Notice where help is needed and be quick to help.
Consider others' perspectives deeply.
Work for peace at many levels.

5. Discover Wisdom.
Cultivate "don't know" mind.
Find connections between Buddhist teachings and your life.
Be open to what arises in every moment.

6. Accept Constant Change.

The Six Right Livelihood Guidelines were developed by members of the BSCW to serve as guidance for informal practice and as a source for contemplation.

Ways to improve your life without trying

I love reading lists of ways to improve your life and even more so when they are virtually effortless ways. Here is a list of 100 ways to slightly improve your life without really trying. My favorite ones are:

- Laugh shamelessly at your own jokes.
- Go for a walk without your phone.
- Learn the names of 10 trees.
- Connect with nature: stand outside barefoot for a few minutes – even when it's cold.
- Get the lighting right: turn off the overhead one, turn on lots of lamps.
- Always be willing to miss the next train.
- Send a voice note instead of a text
- Every so often, search your email for the word "unsubscribe" and then use it on as many as you can.
- Think about your posture: don't slouch, and don't cross your legs.
- Drop your shoulders.
- Always book an extra day off after a holiday.
- Keep a book in your bag to avoid the temptation to doomscroll.
- Listen to the albums you loved as a teenager.
- Make a friend from a different generation.

"Do not buy" list

I have a note on my phone titled "Do not buy" list. At the end of each year, I go through all the product links I saved that I didn't buy and ask myself if I still want them. Most are a resounding "No" and then deleted. The list continues to grow and money continues to be saved. The items I still want I'll save to buy for myself when I've reached a personal milestone or anniversary. Every purchase then becomes linked with a positive memory and infused with meaning.

"To attract something that you want, become as joyful as you think that thing would make you."

— Martha Beck

Better way to practice being grateful

I've been practicing gratitude all wrong. Instead of noting what you are grateful for, try "mental subtraction" and think of one positive event or aspect of your life and then mentally take it away. Contemplate what your life would be like without your home, health, job, partner, etc. and the effect of this will be an enhanced sense of appreciation.

Joy on demand

Here is a very simple and effective three-second brain exercise for finding joy — recognize "thin slices of joy" throughout the day.

"Notice the joyful moments in your day, however small, however fleeting. Notice how good it feels to have that first sip of your drink. Or how tasty that first bite of food is. The pleasurable feeling of your skin in warm water when you wash your hands or take a shower. The moment of delight and comfort when you see your friend. These thin slices of joy only last a few seconds but they add up! The more you notice joy, the more you will experience joy in your life."

That's advice by an ex-Google engineer who wrote the book Joy on Demand. He shares more short and simple "joy" exercises here.

"At some point in life the world's beauty becomes enough. You don't need to photograph, paint or even remember it. It is enough."

— Toni Morrison

Happiness trick

This article titled "1 simple trick to be happier"is not clickbait — it's sound advice. It suggests that because your happiness level is more dependent on the frequency of positive events, rather than the intensity, you should be creating a daisy chain of happiness-inducing events all day long.

"Think of some of the small delights that bring you joy — whether it's a certain song, a photo from a gathering with friends, or even a pen that writes like a dream — and try intentionally placing them throughout your day."

Alternative to affirmations

I just learned this concept of pivoting from affirmations to *iffirmations*. Instead of saying to yourself something like "I am confident and strong" you ask yourself "What *if* I am confident and strong?" Asking it in the form of a question forces your brain to search for evidence that this might be true. For me, this works because it conjures images and examples of ways I could be confident or strong or have been in the past, which then elicits positive and encouraging emotions. A lot more effective that affirmations.

An illustration of Happiness

This illustrated insight of happiness from the
More to That newsletter is amazingly accurate
and perspective-shifting.

*"Happiness is the difference between what you have, and
your definition of enough."*

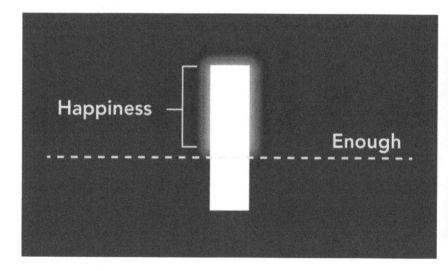

*"If all you did was just looked for things
to appreciate, you would live a joyously
spectacular life."*

– Esther Abraham Hicks

Boost your happiness chemicals

Here's a great list of 100+ hacks for boosting your happiness chemicals. The ones I find most effective are:

Dopamine (reward)
- Create a timeline for your goals to get a clearer vision of your future.
- Schedule something exciting in the future to look forward to
- Share an accomplishment of yours with someone who'd be proud of you.

Oxytocin (love/bonding)
- Use more "we"-language in your relationships.
- Play with a pet (especially a dog or cat).
- Recognize your sense of oneness with everything.

Serotonin (happiness/mood)
- Sunbathe
- Go for a long walk.
- Consume high protein foods such as salmon, turkey, eggs, and nuts.

Endorphins (energy/pain-killer)
- Practice fast and powerful breathing to boost your energy levels.
- Dance to fast and upbeat music.
- Approach new people you want to meet. "10 second relationships" can boost mental health and positive emotions.

"When stumped by a life choice, choose 'enlargement' over happiness."

— James Hollis

Create moments of transcendence

Leo Babauta of Zen Habits wrote a wonderfully succinct post on How to Make the Most of Your 24 Hours. There are 4 things he mentions are:

1. Be intentional at the start of each day
2. Only 3 important tasks: don't shoot for doing more, do what matters
3. Reflect with gratitude
4. Create multiple moments of transcendence throughout your day. Elevate small moments of your life—like cooking or washing dishes—to something special, sacred and alive.

The days I remember the most are not the days I cross everything off my list. It's the days when I slow down and deepen the moments and spaces in between tasks.

Cognitive

"Hey look! I get to create whatever persona I want to, and it's all up to me. And the truth is, we are all basically the universe— pretending to be humans for a brief moment in time.

— RuPaul

Inspiration for Overthinkers

This small, illustrated handbook titled Get Out
of My Head: Inspiration for Overthinkers in an
Anxious World by Meredith Arthur, has become
a roadmap to help me navigate my anxieties and
distortions. It's much more magical than it is
clinical. You can pick it up and start anywhere in the book at
any time, and you'll find playful ways to reframe your thinking
and easy actionable advice to try now.

- TRY: Unspooling your brain by taking a phone-free walk.
  Boredom is a means to an end.
- TRY: Figuring out your energy budget, then spending
  carefully in favor of equilibrium—even if it means letting go
  of something important.
- TRY: Removing a layer of clothing or opening a window
  when you're stuck in your thoughts. See if it brings you back
  into the moment.
- TRY: Paying attention to the absence of a hormone wave and
  figuring out what caused that calm sea.

*"Life is not a problem to be solved, but a
reality to be experienced."*

— Jacobus Johannes van der Leeuw

A tool to measure divergent thinking

I've been using this Divergent Association Task to measure my verbal creativity. It takes less than 2 minutes and involves thinking of 10 words that are as different from each other as possible. The test was designed by a postdoctoral fellow at Harvard, and according to the study — which involved 9,000 participants all over the world — people who are more creative generate words that have greater distances between them.

Unblock your creativity

Here's a visualization to help unblock the creative process by Julian Shapiro. He calls it the "Creativity Faucet":

Visualize your creativity as a backed-up pipe of water. The first mile is packed with wastewater. This wastewater must be emptied before the clear water arrives. ... Let's apply this to creativity: At the beginning of a writing session, write out every bad idea that unavoidably comes to mind. ... Once the bad ideas are emptied, strong ideas begin to arrive.

Here's his explanation of why this works.

188 Cognitive Biases

The Cognitive Bias Codex is a useful and informative radial diagram of 188 cognitive biases listed on Wikipedia. All the biases are grouped into categories and each one links to its own Wikipedia page where you can learn more.

"Your assumptions are your windows on the world. Scrub them off every once in a while, or the light won't come in."

— Isaac Asimov

9 common thinking biases

I'm sure I'm afflicted by a lot of cognitive biases, but I like this list of 9 common biases, because of the short advice on how to overcome them. I'll admit that I struggle with the halo effect — "when your overall impression of someone is influenced by one part of their character" — but I'm working on it and learning to appreciate humans in all their complexities.

9 Common Thinking Biases
and how to overcome them

by @inner_drive | www.innerdrive.co.uk

Confirmation Bias

What it is: Paying more attention to people or ideas that you agree with.

Overcoming it: Talk to a diverse range of people before you make a decision.

Halo Effect

What it is: Your overall impression of someone is influenced by one part of their character.

Overcoming it: Remember that first impressions may not be the most accurate.

Hawthorne Effect

What it is: If someone knows that they are being observed or monitored, it can alter their behaviour.

Overcoming it: Take a long term approach and make observations of others as discrete as possible.

Negativity Bias

What it is: You pay more attention to and remember things that are negative.

Overcoming it: Take time to actively reflect on the good things that have happened.

Bandwagon Effect

What it is: You tend to believe things more when other people do.

Overcoming it: Listen to your gut. What would your opinion be if you didn't know anyone else's?

Dunning Kruger Effect

What it is: Unskilled people overestimate their ability and experts doubt themselves.

Overcoming it: Take anyone who makes definitive 100% statements with a pinch of salt.

Ikea Effect

What it is: You place a disproportionately high value on the things that you personally create or assemble.

Overcoming it: Just because it's your idea doesn't make it a good one. Know when to cut your losses.

Outcome Bias

What it is: Judging your decision based on the outcome, instead of the quality of decision when it was made.

Overcoming it: Take time to reflect on what information you had at the time and if you would do anything differently.

Planning Fallacy

What it is: Under-estimating how long it will take you to complete a task.

Overcoming it: Give yourself more time than you think. Start earlier.

Social media distortions

It's been more than three years since I deleted my Facebook account and lately, I find myself using Instagram and Twitter less and less. This list of 8 Ways Social Media Distorts Reality by the Center for Humane Technology reminded me why I have a 5-minute time limit on my social media apps. I'm especially sensitive to "information flooding" and the algorithms are great at tricking me into thinking that everyone is talking about this *one* thing. As much as I do appreciate a community, I have to remind myself that Twitter and Instagram are not reality. The entire list is worth reading and understanding.

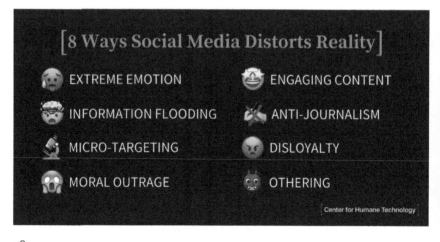

[8 Ways Social Media Distorts Reality]

EXTREME EMOTION

ENGAGING CONTENT

INFORMATION FLOODING

ANTI-JOURNALISM

MICRO-TARGETING

DISLOYALTY

MORAL OUTRAGE

OTHERING

Center for Humane Technology

List of common misconceptions

I'm learning a lot from scrolling through this list of common misconceptions. These are concise summaries that are linked to longer articles on Wikipedia. I like that they are worded as a correction, with the misconceptions implied. I'm relieved to dispel the misconception that the pyramids of Egypt were built by slave labor. I've learned that dogs sweat mainly through their footpads and the Pacific Tree Frog is the only frog species that actually makes the "ribbit" sound.

Reframe your decision-making process

According to "Why Emotionally Intelligent People Embrace the 2-Way-Door Rule to Make Better and Faster Decisions," we avoid making decisions because we assume most are one-way door decisions, meaning irreversible, like quitting your job. In reality, most decisions are two-way door decisions where the door swings both ways, so if you step through and don't like what you see, you can always turn around and go back through. Once you recognize this difference, you'll find you actually seek out opportunities to make more decisions.

How to stop worrying about what other people think

Here is a positive visual that shows you ways to stop worrying about what other people think. My favorite tactic is to "Remember that people aren't that interested in you." If I ever hesitate sharing something I wrote or created, I just tell myself "No one cares." It's so freeing.

How to quiet your mind chatter

Here is a case for talking to yourself more often. Ethan Kross, experimental psychologist and neuroscientist, suggests that a key strategy for controlling negative thought loops and ruminating is "distanced self-talk" — talking to yourself as if you were another person. This involves calling yourself by name and using non-first pronouns like "you." I like to talk to myself out loud while I'm driving alone. It's a sacred time when I get to ask myself questions, spew out my fragmented thinking and work problems out. I feel confident and safe doing this in the car, because no one can hear me and if anyone sees me they'll just assume I'm on the phone.

HOW TO STOP WORRYING ABOUT WHAT OTHER PEOPLE THINK

Remember that people aren't that interested in you.

They generally don't care about you as much as you think they do. Psychologists call the tendency to overestimate how much other people pay attention to you the "spotlight effect."

Tell yourself a different story.

No one can make you think or feel a certain way — it's all about the way you interpret their behavior. If you fall and people laugh, try telling yourself that you cheered them up instead of focusing on how stupid you are.

Know that it's okay to care what others think.

It's fine to care about your reputation. The key is not letting that concern overwhelm you. Ultimately, you want to care more about what you think of you than what others think of you.

Try to make others comfortable.

We're generally pretty bad at guessing how much others are struggling. Think about what you can do to make their lives easier, and you may find that your personal concerns are less salient.

Focus on controlling your thoughts, not theirs.

Mentally strong people rarely focus on things they can't control — like other people's thoughts. Once you shift your focus away from those things, you'll likely be happier and less stressed.

Don't try to please everyone.

People will always judge you no matter what — so it's foolish to try to look good in everyone's estimation.

Meet more people.

Everyone has a different opinion — one person's negative perception of you doesn't matter that much.

SOURCE: Quora; Journal of Personality and Social Psychology

Emotions

---

*"We waste our energy and
exhaust ourselves with the
insistence that life be otherwise."*
— Frank Ostaseski

What you can control and what you can't

I like this visual reminder I came across on Reddit of "What I can control and what I can't." It reminds me to celebrate the wins — I no longer reactively say, "You make me feel this." Instead I self-correct to say, "When you do this, I feel this."

What I can control and what I can't

Data source: @mindfulenough | Infographic design by @agrassoblog for educational and motivational purposes

OUT OF MY CONTROL

The past

The future

The actions of others

The opinions of others

IN MY CONTROL

What happens around me

What other people think of me

The outcome of my efforts

How others take care of themselves

My boundaries

My thoughts & actions

The goals I set

What I give my energy to

How I speak to myself

How I handle challenges

23

How to Stop
Taking Things Personally

1. Realise that other people's rudeness is not about you. When someone is rude it's likely to be a reflection of their own issues.

2. Ask yourself what else the comment or behaviour might mean. For example, if someone doesn't smile or say hello, they might be shy.

3. Take comments or criticism in a constructive way. Ask yourself if there's any truth to it, and what you can learn.

4. Take a different perspective. Ask yourself how an unbiased outsider would see the situation.

5. Realise that you can't please everyone.

6. Know that you're not defined by your mistakes or criticism.

7. Realise that your self-worth depends on you. It does not depend on what others say about you.

How to stop taking things personally

Sometimes my obstacle is taking something personally that shouldn't be. Like when my husband asks me if I unloaded the dishwasher "yet" and I interpret it as an all-out attack on my productivity. My therapist has advised me to "listen to the request, not the tone." But that's easy to forget.

If you also struggle with the same thing, here's an infographic inspired by this blog post.

←

"*Let everything happen to you: beauty and terror. Just keep going. No feeling is final.*"

— Rainer Maria Rilke

Classify your emotions

I am hoping I'll get better at communicating my emotions by studying this chart of W. Gerrod Parrott's Emotion Classification. It is a mind map of the 6 core emotions we feel and all the other emotions that branch off of them.

→

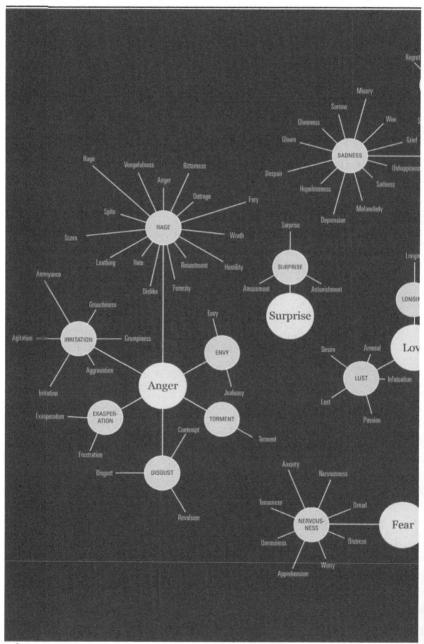

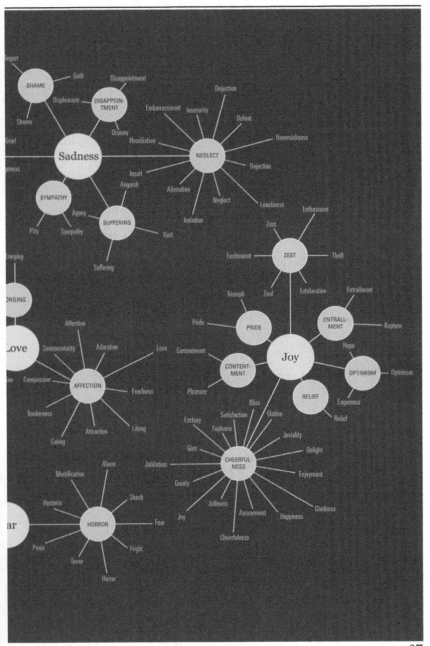

Visual toolkit for grief

Grief Deck is a free visual resource for grief support. Each card you flip over delivers a prompt to focus on and allow your feelings arise. The best advice I ever received regarding grief was to "schedule it" — daily if you need to. For a month, I would hold in my tears until I was alone and then I would cry until I was exhausted. After a month, it became less and less, but I never stop making space for it. Here is the card I contributed, inspired by my father-in-law who we lost in 2020. ⟶

"Life will break you. Nobody can protect you from that, and being alone won't either, for solitude will also break you with its yearning. You have to love. You have to feel. It is the reason you are here on earth. You have to risk your heart. You are here to be swallowed up. And when it happens that you are broken, or betrayed, or left, or hurt, or death brushes too near, let yourself sit by an apple tree and listen to the apples falling all around you in heaps, wasting their sweetness. Tell yourself that you tasted as many as you could."

—Louise Erdrich, The Painted Drum

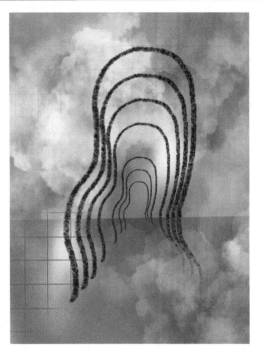

Subliming

We're taught at a young age in school that form is in flux.
Water can change its physical state from solid to liquid to gas
a million times and never lose any part of itself. We forget
this fact in grief. The ones we love die and we forget to sense
their new state of being. We only miss the form which we lost.
We cry and grieve, but somewhere in this realm there is a
hologram, and it is made of love, and it has no physical form —
only feeling — but that feeling is one that heals and integrates
and transcends all sadness. Try to spend some time feeling this
new form.

A tip for taming anger

I remember reading somewhere that customer service desks often times have a mirror mounted behind them so that customers can keep their cool when complaining. I thought of that when I read this quote from by Thich Nhat Hanh from Taming the Tiger Within: Meditations on Transforming Difficult Emotions:

> *Whenever anger comes up, take out a mirror and look at yourself. When you are angry, you are not very beautiful, you are not presentable. Hundreds of muscles on your face become very tense. Your face looks like a bomb ready to explode.*

I don't really pull out a mirror, but when I begin to feel my face get tense I immediately remind myself to relax my jaw and muscles and it helps to temper the hot emotions.

"To get out of your anger, you can close your eyes and visualize the other person in 300 years. What will they become? Ash. And you too."

— Thich Nhat Hanh

Focus

"Make no little plans; they have no magic to stir men's blood and probably themselves will not be realized. Make big plans; aim high in hope and work, remembering that a noble, logical diagram once recorded will never die, but long after we are gone will be a living thing, asserting itself with ever-growing insistency. Remember that our sons and grandsons are going to do things that would stagger us."
— Daniel Burnham

Free focus timer

The Marinara: Pomodoro Assistant
is free timer for your Chrome browser. I use
it when I have trouble focusing. The timer goes
off every 30 minutes and takes over my browser
window for a 7 minute break, but you can
customize the time limits.

Some ideas to focus a wandering mind

This infographic has 9 suggestions for focusing
your wandering mind.

1. Play music without lyrics
2. Allow short breaks to daydream
3. Identify and eliminate stressors
4. Grab a cup of coffee
5. Take 1 minute to doodle
6. Count slowly as your breathe
7. Try a Naam Yoga hand trick
8. Pay attention to what triggers your mind wandering
9. Try chewing gum

$\longrightarrow$

6 COUNT SLOWLY AS YOU BREATHE

Buddhist meditators laud the benefits of breath counting meditation, which is an exercise for the mind that cleanses distracting thoughts and builds concentration power.[6]

HOW TO

Take a slow, deep inhale and pause.

Exhale slowly and count "one."

Repeat to the count of 10.

As you get better, increase the number of breaths.

7 TRY A NAAM YOGA HAND TRICK TO REDUCE STRESS

Author Sharon Melnick suggests applying pressure to the space between your second and third knuckle (index and middle fingers). This activates a nerve near the heart and creates a sense of instant calm, allowing your brain to better control mind wandering.[7]

TRY IT

Up the ante by incorporating **deep breathing**, a critical part of an effective yoga practice.

33

How to take your time back

According to the Michelle Drouin, the behavioral scientist who wrote this article "The Time Hack Everyone Should Know," the key to taking your time back is not a phone detox or monitoring your screen time, it is to remember 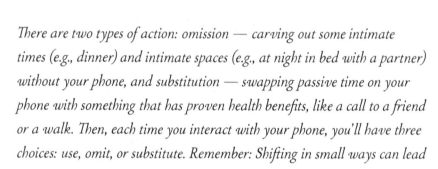 we have the tool of choice (use, omit or substitute) and to have a plan of action ready the next time you reach for your phone.

There are two types of action: omission — carving out some intimate times (e.g., dinner) and intimate spaces (e.g., at night in bed with a partner) without your phone, and substitution — swapping passive time on your phone with something that has proven health benefits, like a call to a friend or a walk. Then, each time you interact with your phone, you'll have three choices: use, omit, or substitute. Remember: Shifting in small ways can lead to big changes in our daily timeclock.

She's right when she says, "Don't deceive yourself into thinking you're being sucked into your technologies. Instead, see your tech use for what it is: you knowing what you like, and you choosing to engage in it (at the cost of other opportunities)." When I take responsibility for my choices is when I'm most motivated to make better choices.

Inner life

---

*"Things usually happen around us,
not to us."*

— Unknown

How to find the right therapist

Here is some great advice on how to find the right therapist. One of the first steps is to figure out what kind of therapeutic framework you need. When I first started therapy I had anxiety that sometimes resulted in panic attacks. Cognitive Behavioral Therapy taught me how to redirect a thought so that it doesn't create overwhelming feelings that would affect my behavior. Now, 8 years later, I have a person-centered therapist that I talk to about all aspects of my life. Each session feels like I'm catching up with my very insightful and intelligent friend who I can vent to and ask for advice. I always tell my friends that you are allowed to break up with your therapist if the fit isn't right. I saw three therapists before I found my most recent one, who I've been seeing for three years now. Finding the "right therapist" feels like you've acquired a super power.

Different types of therapy

Here's a great jumping off point to learn about different types and approaches to psychotherapy. Currently there are 162 different modalities for therapy listed.

Mental health newsletter

The Mental Health Update is one of my favorite newsletters to hit my inbox. There's always a tool or article that widens my perspective. Each issue has actionable strategies to improve your mental health. The newsletter was created by Jordan Brown, a social worker who started blogging because he couldn't find the kind of mental health content online that he wanted to read. I'm always surprised by his articles and what he covers, so I am grateful.

Free confidential crisis line

If you're in the United States and need someone to talk to you can text 741741 any hour of the day and be connected with a crisis counselor (For Canada text 686868, and for UK text 85258). The counselors go through continuous training and are always supervised by mental health professionals. I tested it out to make sure it works and the first text was automated, but I was connected with a live person in less than 2 minutes. I hope I don't need it, but I'm relieved to know that it's there. For more info check out their website: crisistextline.org.

Walking a labyrinth

I find that walking a labyrinth is a much simpler way for me to meditate than sitting. I stand at the entrance and contemplate my issue or question, then after some deep breathing — and when I feel ready — I enter. As I walk through the winding path toward the middle, I imagine myself shedding all fears and doubts, so that when I arrive at the center I physically feel lighter and open for clarity. What I love about walking labyrinths is that the closer you get to the center the farther you are in distance. Which is often how I feel about life.

Create your own vision quest

Eight years ago I went on a vision quest in the Inyo Mountains and it was transformative and one of the best things I've ever done for myself. If you've ever considered going on one or want to learn more about it, I very much recommend the book I read to prepare called Quest: A Guide for Creating Your Own Vision Quest. I might not ever get the guts to go back out there again, but revisiting this book and going through it's exercises is an enlightening journey inward.

"When I notice myself worrying about 'what other people will think' I find I'm usually not worried about any single person's opinion. If I pick a specific person, I'm rarely concerned about what they will think. What I fear is the collective opinion in my head. It's imaginary"

— James Clear

100 wishes on a post-its

I spent some time writing out 100 wishes of mine on post-its inspired by this post: How and Why to do a Life Audit. The idea is to brainstorm your life goals, values, dreams and then categorize them based on themes and timeframes. The process allows for your priorities to come to light and helps you to see the patterns of your life. I could only fill 50 post-its in one sitting and as I discover new dreams of mine I go back to my remaining post-it pack to add more. I found that once I had written down all the desires inside of me and, in a sense, got them out of my system, it freed up space for completely new and weirdly fun wishes to show up.

Imagine your future daily routine

In this Extraordinary Routine interview, Designer/Adventurer Frankie Ratford talks a little bit about how she came to design her life by *"imagining her future daily routine"* and realizing that a desk had no part of it. This got me thinking about how I do the same thing when I let myself daydream and how often my daydreams seem to materialize in my real life. And since there is power in intention, I think this would be a great practice to adopt. Think of it as a mental Pinterest board and practice pinning up all the qualities you want your future day-to-day life to have.

How to do a Life Pie

The Six Spokes Theory or Life Pie is a "strategy for an optimal life" is a great way to draw out a snapshot of your life and see what areas might need more attention. You start by drawing a circle and dividing it into 6 slices. Each slice is assigned to an aspect of your life. You then draw a dot on the dividing line to the degree that you feel fulfilled. After connecting the dots, you'll be able to spot in what areas you are lopsided. I made a short YouTube video outlining my process here.

A case for Nostalgia

In this YouTube video titled "Mindfulness isn't the only powerful mental state," Dr. Clay Routledge makes a case for Nostalgia as a valuable psychological resource that can mobilize and motivate you to find new meaning in life. My favorite way to experience Nostalgia is to, once a month, set aside a night to be alone with my old diaries, birthday cards, letters, pictures and other mementos while listening to music from that time period. Revisiting happy memories of the past strengthens self-continuity, connection and belongingness in the world.

The Alien Exercise

In Jen Sincero's book, You Are a Badass, she describes the Alien Exercise for rebooting yourself and getting some clarity. Imagine you are an alien and you've just landed on Earth — into your body and life. Take notice of all the connections, opportunities, skills, possessions and people who love you and can help you. What would you do and how would you feel? I think this is great for brainstorming projects, ideas and new ways to enjoy your day-to-day life.

"Life shrinks or expands in proportion to one's courage."

— Anaïs Nin

Death reminder app

WeCroak (iOS, Android) is a bit morbid but I love it. At random times throughout the day I get a notification banner that says "Don't forget, you're going to die," which prompts me to open the app for a quote. All the quotes are about dying. The app is inspired by Bhutanese culture where one is expected to think about death five times a day to achieve happiness. Here are some death quotes to contemplate:

- Here is the world: beautiful and terrible things will happen. Don't be afraid. — Frederick Buechner
- And I was some of the mud that got to sit up and look around. Lucky me, lucky mud. — Kurt Vonnegut
- The other side of the "sacred" is the sight of your beloved in the underworld, dripping with maggots." — Gary Snyder
- Let go, live your life, the grave has no sunny corners. — Charles Wright
- Since death is certain, but the time of death is uncertain, what is the most important thing? — Pema Chödrön

Why is it so important for you to have a baby?

Last year I made the very important decision to not have children. This quiz helped me figure out the true reasons I wanted to be a parent and I realized that those reasons were not really aligned with what I want for my life. After that came a lot of reading and therapy before I became confident that this was the best decision I ever made for myself. So in case anyone else is on the fence, here's a good place to start.

An honest book about motherhood

The Female Assumption is a raw and honest look at becoming a mother and the pressures on women to reproduce. I couldn't put it down. Mother of 3, Melanie Holmes interviewed mothers from all over the world to accurately portray what happens behind the curtain of motherhood. She also includes the stories of women who have consciously chosen to not be mothers. This book is a well-balanced pros and cons list for either path, and a reminder that whatever you decide for yourself is the right choice. Every young woman should read this.

Write your own eulogy

Anne-Laure Le Cunff of Ness Labs has a
great post on the exercise of writing your own
eulogy as a blueprint for your future. The
process of writing down the exact values and
accomplishments you want to be remembered for
can provide clarity as to the small steps you can take today to
create that narrative. Her post provides example questions to
help you draft a eulogy and it's up to you to work backwards to
take action.

*"People say that what we're all seeking
is a meaning for life. I don't think that's
what we're really seeking. I think that
what we're seeking is an experience of
being alive, so that our life experiences
on the purely physical plane will have
resonances with our own innermost
being and reality, so that we actually
feel the rapture of being alive."*
— Joseph Campbell

Discover your values in 5 minutes

This Personal Values Assessment takes only 5 minutes to complete and it peers right into your soul. I felt naked after reading the report of what matters to me the most and essentially, what drives my decision-making process. I've been taking this as an end of year test for almost 5 years now. It inspires me to either work on the values I want to change or live closer to what is most important to me.

The Wisdom Index

Researchers at UC San Diego created a 7-question survey that can determine your level of wisdom called the Jeste-Thomas Wisdom Index. You can take the 5-minute test here. The questions relate to 7 components of wisdom: Acceptance of Divergent Perspectives, Decisiveness, Emotional Regulation, Pro-Social Behaviors, Self-Reflection, Social Advising and Spirituality. Wisdom scores range from 1-5 with a score of 3 being considered neutral. My highest score was a 5 in Spirituality and my lowest score was 3.75 in Social Advising.

Nature

"*Nature does not hurry, yet everything is accomplished.*"

— Lao Tzu

Explore the Tree of Life

OneZoom is an interactive tree of life that allows you to zoom in and out and explore the connections between 2.2 million living species. It's a lot to visualize and process, but fun to explore. I felt really small and grateful realizing what a tiny little branch of life we are as humans.

Trees from all over the world

Being able to identify tree species is something I ache to learn but I am intimidated by the amount of field research required, and then I discovered Monumental Trees, a website where people all over the world can submit their tree photos that you can filter by species and country. I still haven't discovered all this site has to offer, but for now just looking at the photos satiates my curiosity.

"The fragrance of flowers is their prayer."
— Bulgarian philosopher Peter Deunov

Largest database on rocks and minerals

Mindat.org is a great website to lose time if you're an amateur rockhound. It is a nonprofit project by The Hudson Institute of Mineralogy, and the "leading authority on minerals and their localities, deposits, and mines worldwide." There's a lot of ways to search for and discover new rocks, including a search by color. If you're more of a "pro" than an amateur you can contribute your own photos and data. My husband likes to bring home rocks from river beds and hikes and I gravitate more toward crystals, but it's one thing to admire the natural beauty and wonder of our earth's materials and another to learn about it's importance and use in our world.

Get lost in the clouds

Everything you could ever want to know about clouds is available at the International Cloud Atlas hosted by the World Meteorological Organization. You can learn the basics of observing and identifying clouds. See photo descriptions of clouds. Search their image gallery and compare images.

Learn from Nature

Asknature.org is a free online tool where you can search thousands of nature's solutions to various challenges. Like how a decentralized society helps ants to recover from a food shortage or how maple tree seeds twirl in a tornado-like vortex to increase the reach of where their seeds are planted. Just ten minutes a day exploring this website will get you thinking differently.

Nature live cams

For a dose of awe and wonder head over to Explore.org and choose from almost 100 live nature cams available at any time. There's ocean cams, bears, gorillas, puppies and kittens and other animal sanctuaries. Never a dull moment.

A timeline of food

This fascinating food timeline outlines the beginning of food, beginning with water & ice, and includes ancient recipes throughout time. It was created by a Food History Librarian who started her project in 1999 and continues to update it.

Timeline of the Human Condition

Here is a long scroll through milestones in
human evolution, sourced from Wikipedia,
Encyclopaedia Britannica, and BBC, and put
together by a Professor in Ecology. At the end
of the page there is a note of Ages that rescales
the timeline to a calendar year which is really interesting. The
Big Bang begins on January 1, the Sun forming on September
1, earliest signs of life appear on September 13, and just 2 hours
before the year's end appears us — humans.

Fascinating physical visualizations

I love poring over this gallery of physical
visualizations. Each artifact is a representation
of data from our history dating back to
Mesopotamian Clay Tokens from 5500 BC.
Some of them are so interesting and beautiful,
like the brainwave weaving of dreamers, or
the Yakima Time Ball meant to record major life events. Others
are useful like an abacus ring from the Qing Dynasty, or
mysterious, like South American Quipus. There are currently
370 artifacts listed — all of them equally captivating.

Reading tools

"When you reach the end of what you know, you will be at the beginning of what you should sense."

— Kahlil Gibran

Find out how long to read any book

Before you pick the next book on your reading list you should check out How Long to Read. Their search engine includes more than 12 million books and their speed reading timer will calculate approximately how long it will take you to read the book in its entirety.

Remember what you read

If you read books on Kindle or iBooks you should be using Readwise. Every passage I highlight in my Kindle is auto-imported and sent back to me in a thrice-weekly email (you can choose the frequency and number of highlights you receive). I also have it synced to my Evernote account, so that anytime new highlights are imported, my Evernote is updated immediately. Using Readwise makes me want to read more and highlight more, I've even started scanning the highlighted passages from my favorite paper books.

You can read a random selection of my highlights at readwise.io/@claudia

Four different ways to read books

The Curious Reader has a great outline of the 4 different reading levels and sub-types pulled from "How to Read a Book."

The first level being Elementary Reading
— where the main question of reading is "What does the sentence say?"

Level two is Inspectional — where you ask, "What is the book/article about?" This is how I read most news articles and blog posts.

Level three is Analytical — when you want to really understand the topic by asking questions and chewing and digesting it.

The fourth level of reading is my favorite: Syntopic Reading. This is where you read multiple books on the same subject and compare and contrast the ideas.

Each reading level serves a different purpose, so it's helpful to ask yourself before reading, "What do I want out of this book or article?"

Elegant bookmark

I was coveting this Swedish anchor
bookmark back when it was just a Kickstarter
and this year I finally bought one for myself. The
Page Anchor is made from 316L stainless steel and
weighs about 8 ounces and has only one purpose
— to hold a book open perfectly flat. The craftsmanship is so
beautiful that it feels like owning a piece a jewelry.

Inconspicuous bookmarks

Levenger Page Nibs make all other page markers
look primitive. They are beautifully made —
stamped and made of copper. You just slide one on
to the page and click it into place. They are paper
thin and won't damage your books. I find these
are so useful for marking recipe pages, and passages I want to
scan.

*"Don't make something unless it is both
necessary and useful; but if it is both
necessary and useful, don't hesitate to
make it beautiful." Philosophy*

–The Shaker Design

Relationships

---

*"'You are partly right' — When
someone congratulates you or
criticizes you, you can use this
mantra."*
— Thich Nhat Hanh

Relationship mini-insight

In this short snippet from a longer interview, Esther Perel explains "Why your Partner Criticizes You." She says behind every criticism is a wish. This does not excuse being critical toward your partner, but keeping this in mind helps me focus on what it is I'm really requesting of my partner and what he might be asking of me. Worth the 4-minute listen.

"You're under no obligation to be the same person you were 5 minutes ago."

– Alan Watts

Cool down phrases ⟶

This Gottman Institute blog post has some examples of phrases to help de-escalate arguments with your partner. I wish it wasn't so hard to say "I'm sorry" when I'm in the wrong, but these workarounds help steer heated conversations back on track.

Gottman Repair Checklist

I Feel

1. I'm getting scared.
2. Please say that more gently.
3. Did I do something wrong?
4. That hurt my feelings.
5. That felt like an insult.
6. I'm feeling sad.
7. I feel blamed. Can you rephrase that?
8. I'm feeling unappreciated.
9. I feel defensive. Can you rephrase that?
10. Please don't lecture me.
11. I don't feel like you understand me right now.
12. Sounds like it's all my fault.
13. I feel criticized. Can you rephrase that?
14. I'm getting worried.
15. Please don't withdraw.

Sorry

1. My reactions were too extreme. Sorry.
2. I really blew that one.
3. Let me try again.
4. I want to be gentler to you right now and I don't know how.
5. Tell me what you hear me saying.
6. I can see my part in all this.
7. How can I make things better?
8. Let's try that one over again.
9. What you are saying is...
10. Let me start again in a softer way.
11. I'm sorry. Please forgive me.

Get to Yes

1. You're starting to convince me.
2. I agree with part of what you're saying.
3. Let's compromise here.
4. Let's find our common ground.
5. I never thought of things that way.
6. This problem is not very serious in the big picture.
7. I think your point of view makes sense.
8. Let's agree to include both our views in a solution.
9. What are your concerns?

I Need to Calm Down

1. Can you make things safer for me?
2. I need things to be calmer right now.
3. I need your support right now.
4. Just listen to me right now and try to understand.
5. Tell me you love me.
6. Can I have a kiss?
7. Can I take that back?
8. Please be gentler with me.
9. Please help me calm down.
10. Please be quiet and listen to me.
11. This is important to me. Please listen.
12. I need to finish what I was saying.
13. I am starting to feel flooded.
14. Can we take a break?
15. Can we talk about something else for a while?

Stop Action!

1. I might be wrong here.
2. Please let's stop for a while.
3. Let's take a break.
4. Give me a moment. I'll be back.
5. I'm feeling flooded.
6. Please stop.
7. Let's agree to disagree here.
8. Let's start all over again.
9. Hang in there. Don't withdraw.
10. I want to change the topic.
11. We are getting off track.

I Appreciate

1. I know this isn't your fault.
2. My part of this problem is...
3. I see your point.
4. Thank you for...
5. That's a good point.
6. We are both saying...
7. I understand.
8. I love you.
9. I am thankful for...
10. One thing I admire about you is...
11. I see what you're talking about.
12. This is not your problem, it's OUR problem.

Short meditations on Love

I bought How to Love by Thich Nhat Hanh on Kindle, read it in one sitting, and often go back to it for short, helpful reminders on how to be more loving. Two of my favorite passages are:

- *"You are part of the universe; you are made of stars. When you look at your loved one, you see that he is also made of stars and carries eternity inside. Looking in this way, we naturally feel reverence."*
- *"There's a tradition in Asia of treating your partner with the respect you would accord a guest. This is true even if you have been with your loved one for a long time."*

Healthy relationships chart   ⟶

I want to print this chart out wallet-size, laminate it, and hand it out to all the young people in my life who are starting out in new relationships. It lists all the values and traits needed to maintain a healthy relationship, as well as examples of what that might look like. Graphic by Jen Moff.

Healthy Relationships

Acountability

- Admits mistakes (or when wrong)
- Accepts responsibility for behaviors, attitudes, & values

Trust

- Accepting each others word
- Giving the benefit of the doubt

Safety

- Refusing to intimidate or manipulate
- Respecting physical space
- Expressing self non-violently

RESPECT

Cooperation

- Asking not expecting
- Accepting change
- Making decisions together
- Willing to compromise
- Win win resolutions to conflict

Honesty

- Communicates openly and truthfully

Support

- Support each others choices
- Being understanding
- Offering encouragement
- listening non-judgmentally
- Valuing opinions

thejenmoff.com

Find your apology language

I consider myself well-versed in figuring out people's love languages, but I was surprised to find out that there was such a thing as an apology language. I took this free quiz and discovered that I am most receptive of apologies that "Accept Responsibility" meaning simply saying "I was wrong." The other types of apology languages are "Genuinely Repent," "Expressing Regret," "Make Restitution," and "Request Forgiveness."

Empathy explainer video

Here is a cute animated video that shows you the difference between empathy and sympathy and is narrated by Brené Brown. The four qualities of empathy are:

1. Perspective taking.
2. Staying out of judgement.
3. Recognizing emotion in another person.
4. And then communicating that you recognize their emotion.

Something to keep in mind is that rarely does an empathic response begin with the word *"At least..."*

"Understanding a person's hunger and responding to it is one of the most potent tools you'll ever discover for getting through to anyone you meet in business or your personal life."

— Mark Goulston

How to comfort someone

I think being able to make someone feel better is an essential skill and one that I often fail at when I go into problem-solving mode too soon. This article outlines The Four States of Distress:

1. Shocked. 2. Feeling bad and not wanting to feel better. 3. Ready to feel better. 4. Feeling better and needing solutions. — and suggests the most helpful actions you can take to comfort someone at each state, depending on their "comfort language." Some of which are:

- Optimism and reframing (e.g., seeing it in a less negative light or finding a silver lining)
- Physical comforting (e.g., a hug)
- Validating their emotions
- Distraction (e.g., doing a fun activity)
- Helping them explore and understand their feelings
- Problem-solving (especially if there is a way to quickly fix much of the problem)

Rules for "fighting"

Here is a list of rules to keep in mind the next time you find yourself faced with a conflict.

Fair Fighting Rules

* Before you begin, ask yourself why you are upset.
* Discuss one issue at a time.
* No degrading language.
* Express your feeling with words and take responsibility for them.
* Take turns talking.
* No stonewalling.
* No yelling.
* Take a time-out if things get too heated.
* Attempt to come to a compromise or an understanding (Segal & Smith, 2015).

P. Greeff, Tanya De Bruyne, A. (2000). *Conflict management style and marital satisfaction. Journal of Sex & Marital Therapy, 26(4), 321-334.*

"Always remember that to argue, and win, is to break down the reality of the person you are arguing against. It is painful to lose your reality, so be kind, even if you are right."

—Haruki Murakami

Research

"Shrink the quantum of experience: instead of reading a book, read a wikipedia article. Instead of eating a cup of ice cream, eat a spoonful. Decreases turnaround time, which both reduces procrastination and also allows me to decide whether I want to go deeper."

— Noah Tye

Ask a Librarian

Library of Congress, the largest library in the world offers free research assistance by experts. I finally had an excuse to use their service and was blown away by how helpful they were. I had been reading History of the Conquest of Mexico written in 1890, and could not find any information for one of the cited sources which was written 300 years prior, so I submitted a request and — in less than 24 hours — I received a response from the Hispanic Division Reference Librarian who linked me to a digitized copy of the manuscript, and 5 other links to codices of Pre-Hispanic History that I would have never discovered otherwise. It's such an invaluable resource.

Get oldest Google search results first

Oldestsearch.com reverse-orders all Google search results so that you see the oldest webpages first. This is refreshing to use, because so often I feel like all the top search results are repetitive.

Search research papers for a consensus

Consensus.app is a search engine that extracts, aggregates and distills findings from 200 million peer-reviewed scientific research papers to answer your questions. It's still in beta, so there is disclaimer that the results are not meant to be taken as final truth, but more of a reflection of relevant research relating to your query. I love using other search engines besides Google whenever I can.

We hear and apprehend only what we already half know.

— Henry David Thoreau

A better search engine for Reddit

I never had any success searching Reddit directly, so I use Google and append all my queries with site:reddit.com. Redditle.com is exactly that — only a simpler, more direct way to search Reddit. You can even search within a specific subreddit.

Find what you didn't know you were looking for

I love the serendipitous search results I get when using Marginalia. It is not equipped to answer questions and suggests that you "instead try to imagine some text that might appear in the website you are looking for, and search for that." SEO-optimized sites are down-ranked and text-heavy sites are favored. If there is a concept or subject I am curious about this search engine will redirect me to blog posts and old personal websites — all of which are never disappointing and always interesting. It's given me such a larger window to the internet.

"If you can see your path laid out in front of you step by step, you know it's not your path. Your own path you make with every step you take. That's why it's your path."
— Joseph Campbell

Self-care

"Be messy and complicated and afraid and show up anyways."
— Glennon Doyle Melton

"Each moment is a place you've never been."
—Mark Strand

Best meditation music

There's rarely a day that goes by that I don't listen to my Meditative Mind: Music & Sleep app. There are hundreds and hundreds of soothing and immersive soundscapes, chants, mantras, nature sounds and world music to choose from. I use it when I need to focus, meditate or sleep. The app is free to download and try out, but I happily pay the $38 annual fee for

access to their full library, unlimited downloads and an ad-free experience. There is also a YouTube channel with long-format music tracks added almost daily.

Quickly de-stress with deep breathing

Doing breathing exercises are easier for me if I can focus on something visually. Xhalr.com is perfect for that. It's also helpful if you want to discover different types of yoga breathing.

60-second worry soother

Pixel Thoughts is a simple website that just wants to help. Type whatever you're stressed about into the star and watch it fade away into the universe, while relaxing music is played and you're reminded that everything will be okay. For me it is most effective on desktop in full-screen mode, but there is an app too.

Beautifully-designed mood tracker

I stopped using mood tracking apps a while back, because I got better at recognizing slight mood shifts and anticipating my own needs in the moment — whether that's asking for space, taking a screen break, or hugging my dog. But now I'm back on the mood tracking app bandwagon, because How We Feel is more than just a mood tracker — it's created by scientists, therapists, designers and engineers, so not only does it help you find the right word for your feelings, it helps you understand the science behind emotions and provides strategies to regulate your mood with elegantly produced videos, and the analytics of your mood over time are displayed in beautifully-designed patterns and colors.

Pain management tactic

I love Brené Brown's exercise of repeating *"Pain, pain, pain, pain, pain,"* to instantly release yourself of the fight or flight mentality. I first heard it in her Men, Women, and Worthiness talk.

"Some people have a lot farther to go from where they begin to get where they want to be—a long way up the mountain, and that is how it has been for me. I don't feel I am getting older; I feel I am getting closer."

—D.H. Lawrence

Self-care checklist ⟶

It can be very hard to check in with yourself when you are feeling anxious or having a bad day. This is a very simple and useful checklist for self-care that I found floating around the internet. Dancing to upbeat music often helps me get out of my head and energized again.

Everything Is Awful and I'm Not Okay: questions to ask before giving up

Are you hydrated?
If not, have a glass of water.

Have you eaten in the past three hours?
If not, get some food — something with protein, not just simple carbs. Perhaps some nuts or hummus?

Have you showered in the past day?
If not, take a shower right now.

Have you stretched your legs in the past day?
If not, do so right now. If you don't have the energy for a run or trip to the gym, just walk around the block, then keep walking as long as you please. If the weather's crap, drive to a big box store (e.g. Target) and go on a brisk walk through the aisles you normally skip.

Have you said something nice to someone in the past day?
Do so, whether online or in person. Make it genuine; wait until you see something really wonderful about someone, and tell them about it.

Have you moved your body to music in the past day?
If not, jog for the length of an EDM song at your favorite tempo, or just dance around the room for the length of an upbeat song.

Have you cuddled a living being in the past two days?
If not, do so. Don't be afraid to ask for hugs from friends or friends' pets. Most of them will enjoy the cuddles too; you're not imposing on them.

Have you seen a therapist in the past few days?
If not, hang on until your next therapy visit and talk through things then.

Have you changed any of your medications in the past couple of weeks, including skipped doses or a change in generic prescription brand?
That may be screwing with your head. Give things a few days, then talk to your doctor if it doesn't settle down.

If daytime: are you dressed?
If not, put on clean clothes that aren't pajamas. Give yourself permission to wear something special, whether it's a funny t-shirt or a pretty dress.

If nighttime: are you sleepy and fatigued but resisting going to sleep?
Put on pajamas, make yourself cozy in bed with a teddy bear and the sound of falling rain, and close your eyes for fifteen minutes — no electronic screens allowed. If you're still awake after that, you can get up again; no pressure.

Do you feel ineffective?
Pause right now and get something small completed, whether it's responding to an e-mail, loading up the dishwasher, or packing your gym bag for your next trip. Good job!

Do you feel unattractive?
Take a goddamn selfie. Your friends will remind you how great you look, and you'll help fight society's restrictions on what beauty can look like.

Do you feel paralyzed by indecision?
Give yourself ten minutes to sit back and figure out a game plan for the day. If a particular decision or problem is still being a roadblock, simply set it aside for now, and pick something else that seems doable. Right now, the important part is to break through that stasis, even if it means doing something trivial.

Have you over-exerted yourself lately — physically, emotionally, socially, or intellectually?
That can take a toll that lingers for days. Give yourself a break in that area, whether it's physical rest, taking time alone, or relaxing with some silly entertainment.

Have you waited a week?
Sometimes our perception of life is skewed, and we can't even tell that we're not thinking clearly, and there's no obvious external cause. It happens. Keep yourself going for a full week, whatever it takes, and see if you still feel the same way then.

You've made it this far, and you will make it through. **You are stronger than you think.**

Get comfortable with uncertainty

I've owned Comfortable with Uncertainty:
108 Teachings on Cultivating Fearlessness and
Compassion by Pema Chödrön for years but
during the pandemic it got pulled off the shelf
more than ever before. You don't need to be a
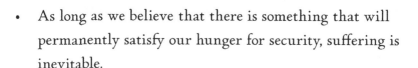
meditation expert or Buddhist to appreciate the message. Each
chapter is a short lesson in self-compassion and awareness,
designed to make you comfortable with uncertainty. It is one of
those books you can open to any page and find wisdom.

- As long as we believe that there is something that will
  permanently satisfy our hunger for security, suffering is
  inevitable.
- In order to be gentle and create an atmosphere of compassion
  for yourself, it's necessary to stop talking to yourself about
  how wrong everything is—or how right everything is, for
  that matter.
- When we don't act out and we don't repress, our passion, our
  aggression, and our ignorance become our wealth. We don't
  have to transform anything. Simply letting go of the story
  line is what it takes, which is not all that easy.

"Let go or be dragged."

— Zen Proverb

Strikethrough stress note

I started a "stress note" in my Notes app where I keep a list of whatever I'm anxious about. Whenever I add something new to the list I first reread my past worries and if they no longer matter (which is usually the case), instead of deleting them I apply the strikethrough style. There is something very calming and self-affirming in doing this, and as the list grows I actually find it very beautiful to look at my past stressors. It reminds me of how resilient I can be.

Worry about it later list

I keep a sticky note on my laptop and when something is bugging me I add it to the list and mentally shelve it until later. By the end of the day most of it doesn't matter and then I get to manually cross it out and that's always satisfying.

Somatic

"When you let go of who you wish
you were, you reclaim your power
to be radiantly, magnetically, and
creatively who you are."
— HeatherAsh Amara

How to return your eyes to their natural state

Here is a tip from the r/Meditation subreddit. To block out your internal monologue practice expanding your peripheral vision. The trick is to keep your vision as "open" as possible, and not to focus on anything unless it's necessary for a specific task. Here is a YouTube video titled: Meditation - Returning Your Eyes to the Natural State, where Meditation teacher Loch Kelly walks you through this exercise. When I practice this an instant calmness washes over me.

Relax your jaw

Every once in awhile I will be scrolling through Reddit and come across a short reminder or tip post that simply says: *Relax your jaw.* I'm not sure at what moment it became second nature to me, but now I instinctively relax my jaw at the first sign of anxiety or discomfort, which is great, because I then drop my shoulders and check-in with my entire body, and just that in itself is an instant mood booster. So I would like to pay it forward with a reminder to *relax your jaw.*

Different types of rest

This TED article outlines the 7 types of rest you
might need and how to go about getting it. The 7
types are: *physical, mental, sensory, creative, emotional,
social, and spiritual.* Obvious advice would be to
make sure you are carving out time for exercise,
sleeping, screen-breaks, nature, and meditation. But two types of
rest that I've never had words for are *emotional rest* and *social rest.*
Emotional rest is giving yourself time and space to freely express
your feelings. (I think my twice-monthly therapy sessions satisfies
this.) And social rest is experienced when you spend time with
positive and supportive people that "revive" you, and stay away
from the relationships that drain you of energy.

Float tank therapy

One of my favorite ways to meditate is inside a
sensory deprivation tank. The sensation of being
weightless helps me detach from my thoughts.
After each session I find myself walking out
deeply relaxed, with zero tension in my body and
a slightly-high feeling. And I sleep deeply afterward. Find a
float station near you.

"What do we live for, if it is not to make life less difficult for each other?"

— George Eliot

Fall asleep faster

Sticking one bare foot outside of the covers helps to initiate a cooling down process which signals to the brain and body that it's time for bed, which can help some people to fall asleep. I try this tactic when I wake up in the middle of the night and it helps me quickly fall back asleep.

Wake up earlier, naturally

I wasn't sure if I would like the Philips Wake-Up Light Alarm Clock, but in one month it's trained me to wake up earlier, naturally. I set the alarm for the time I want to wake up and the light gradually increases beginning about 20 minutes before the alarm is set to go off. During that time is when I usually wake up. When the wake-up light doesn't work, I get woken up by the gentle sounds of birds chirping. Either way, I'm never startled or grumpy.

Nighttime note taking

Before bed every night, I unload whatever is on my mind onto a phone note — which includes everything from work tasks, ideas, shopping lists, anxieties and fears, to things I want to look up on the internet (tomorrow). This keeps my mind clear, my hands off my phone and helps ease me into sleep.

Most common dreams by country

My best friend called recently to ask what it meant to dream her teeth were falling out. I told her that was the most common dream scenario across the board and then asked her more questions about her recent career change, because it was obvious she was nervous about it. Today I came across this infograph showing the most common dreams by country and realized I was partially right — the most googled dream in the world is about snakes, and the second being teeth falling out. I loved learning the other dream meanings being googled in other countries. In Bhutan, they often dream of rainbows.

→

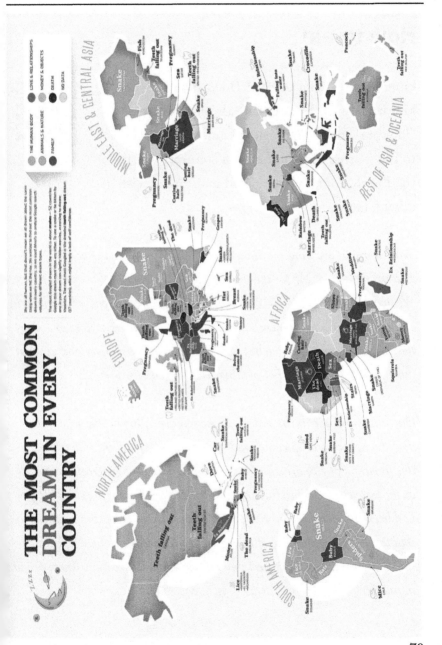

How to eat

I am enjoying Zen teacher Thich Nhat Hanh's Mindfulness Essentials series of small "How to" books. Right now I am reading How to Eat — short meditations on connecting with the Earth, enjoying your food and eating with others. Here are two excerpts:

Wait without waiting — *Standing in line at grocery store or a restaurant, or waiting for the time to eat, we don't need to waste our time. We don't need to "wait" for one second. Instead, we can enjoy breathing in and out for our nourishment and healing. We can use that time to notice that we will soon be able to have food, and we can be happy and grateful during that time. Instead of waiting, we can generate joy.*

Our ancestors are in the soil — *In the soil are many people who have died, have been transformed, and have become part of the soil. Maybe in this mouthful of rice are also the bones of hundreds of generations as well as many leaves, worms and animal's bones. Maybe in a previous life you had been there and died there, and your own bones have disintegrated in that land. During the time of eating, your practice is to look deeply into that grain of rice and enjoy all that has gone into its creation. There are so many things to enjoy and to discover in each bite.*

Mindful eating tip

Putting my fork down between bites helps me slow down, relax while eating and I enjoy my food more. I'm always satisfied without ever feeling "full."

"The goal of life is to make your heartbeat match the beat of the universe, to match your nature with Nature."

— Joseph Campbell

Cooking Meditation

I came across this lovely intention for preparing a meal by Musician Regina Spektor. She shared that she has trouble sitting still and meditating, so this is an active meditation:

You decide something you dedicate the meal to. It can be peace in the world, or someone's health, or anything that is stirring you at the time. Then as you cook, every little action of the cooking—washing, cutting, mixing—can be imbued with that dedication. You concentrate on that intention from start to finish and keep repeating the thought in your mind as you cook. In the end, every bite is filled with that wish.

Productivity

"The cradle rocks above an abyss,
and common sense tells us that
our existence is but a brief crack
of light between two eternities of
darkness."

— Vladimir Nabokov

Favorite to-do list notebook

Two things have kept my to-do list on track
lately. The first is the Maruman Mnemosyne
N197A Today's Act Notebook. I buy them in bulk.
And the second is asking myself the following
questions when planning my day: "What's
the most important thing I can do today that would make
tomorrow better?" and "Should I do this task now or can I do it
later?"

*"When you are making plans, you are
actually not making plans but you are
creating reality..."*

—Unknown on Reddit

A notepad that follows you

My favorite chrome extension is Mindful. It's just
one single note page that you can access in your
browser any time you create a new tab. It's so
useful to instantly have a space to write out tasks,
take quick notes, or collect links. Everything I
type autosaves and syncs to my Chrome Google account so I can
access my notes on both my desktop and laptop.

Tension is who you think you should be.
Relaxation is who you are.

—Chinese proverb

Reduce and organize tab clutter

I use OneTab to close and save all the open tabs that I have an emotional attachment to, but that eat up memory. OneTab is a free chrome extension that converts all my open tabs into a list of links that I can later restore individually or as a group. I love that I can drag and group links and then name them, as well as share them as a webpage. The only inconvenience is that my OneTab doesn't sync across devices, but after a day of working on one device, I just email myself the webpage of closed tabs and that works well enough for me.

Read only what you want

The Just Read chrome extension blocks pop-ups and makes ad-smothered webpages easy on the eyes. You can select and isolate the text you want to read, delete elements, customize styling and print. I use it daily.

Open all links at once

With the Linkclump extension I can drag and select all the links on one page and open them up all at once. It's a real timesaver when I'm proofreading and need to make sure all the embedded links redirect to the right places.

Organize multiple window screens

Magnet is a window manager for Mac that lets me quickly resize and organize up to 4 windows per screen using keyboard shortcuts. It is a must-have productivity tool and it's only 2.99.

Gmail reverse conversation

This chrome extension does only one thing: reverses my Gmail thread view so that the newest message is always on top. Which is the way it should be. No more scrolling or collapsing old messages to get to the most recent.

Chrome extension for using multiple Gmail accounts

I have multiple Gmail accounts that I use throughout the day and I developed a bad habit of keeping them open and constantly clicking through tabs to check the status of my inbox even though I know nothing's changed. Checker Plus is a chrome extension that notifies you of new email so you can preview, delete, star and archive email without opening up Gmail or leaving your current window. It works with multiple accounts.

Multiple inboxes

I use Gmail in my browser, and what I find most helpful is the Multiple Inboxes lab. When I'm working on a project, I create a label for all relevant email and that label becomes an additional inbox. That way, I don't lose sight of my to-dos by placing them in a folder, and it keeps my inbox from becoming cluttered. It has simplified my workflow. Here are instructions.

Visualize your to-do list

This task-mapping tool called Baller ToDo is inspired by the Eisenhower "Urgent-Important" decision making matrix and will help you visualize and figure out the stuff that really matters and most importantly, what you can put off.

① Do First

First focus
on important tasks
to be done the same day.

② Schedule

Important, but
not-so-urgent stuff
should be scheduled.

③ Delegate

What's urgent,
but less important,
delegate to others.

④ Don't Do

What's neither urgent
nor important,
don't do at all.

Top-voted productivity hacks

50hacks.co is a crowdsourced lists of the best productivity hacks written and upvoted by users. No account is necessary to contribute, just scroll to the bottom and click on "+ Add Hack." Here are some of the most upvoted hacks of all time:

- Send yourself an email at the end of the day on Friday with a short list of priorities to get started on come Monday morning. Don't overthink it - just the top half a dozen things on your mind.
- If you want to change, start with the type of content you consume.
- Slow-mo your life. What that means is that whatever activity you are doing, slow down your movement. You'll notice an immediate calming effect; your brain starts to process things better, you begin to appreciate the little details in your environment that you never noticed before.
- The second you're at your desk knock out the task that you dread the most. Do this every single day.
- Chain your habits together one after the other, so that one habit is sort of triggering the next for a productive day.

"We're in a freefall into future. We don't know where we're going. Things are changing so fast, and always when you're going through a long tunnel, anxiety comes along. And all you have to do to transform your hell into a paradise is to turn your fall into a voluntary act. It's a very interesting shift of perspective and that's all it is... joyful participation in the sorrows and everything changes."

—Joseph Campbell

Productive hacks visual

I will never hesitate to click on an article about productivity, because I always hope to discover at least one new way of looking at things. Here is an infographic titled How to Be Productive. In this case, it was "Assume you are right, when in doubt. Decisive is productive." That makes sense to me.

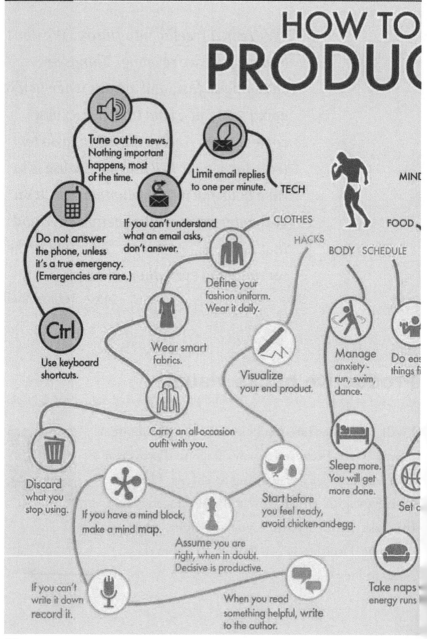

HOW TO
PRODUC

Tune out the news. Nothing important happens, most of the time.

Limit email replies to one per minute.

TECH

If you can't understand what an email asks, don't answer.

Do not answer the phone, unless it's a true emergency. (Emergencies are rare.)

CLOTHES

HACKS

MIND

FOOD

BODY **SCHEDULE**

Define your fashion uniform. Wear it daily.

Ctrl

Use keyboard shortcuts.

Wear smart fabrics.

Visualize your end product.

Manage anxiety - run, swim, dance.

Do ea: things f

Carry an all-occasion outfit with you.

Discard what you stop using.

If you have a mind block, make a mind map.

Start before you feel ready, avoid chicken-and-egg.

Sleep more. You will get more done.

Set c

Assume you are right, when in doubt. Decisive is productive.

If you can't write it down record it.

When you read something helpful, write to the author.

Take naps energy runs

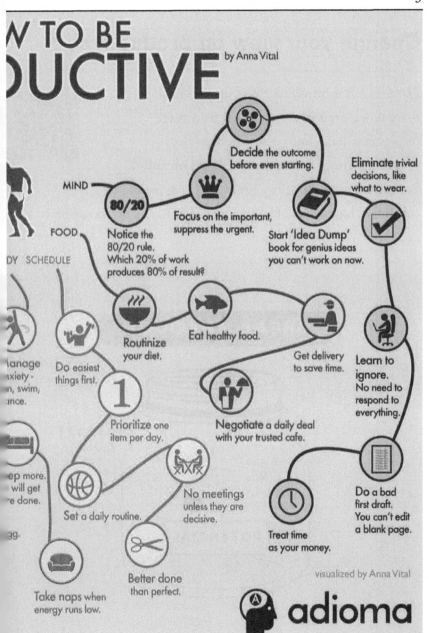

N TO BE
DUCTIVE by Anna Vital

MIND

FOOD

DY SCHEDULE

80/20

Decide the outcome before even starting.

Eliminate trivial decisions, like what to wear.

Focus on the important, suppress the urgent.

Notice the 80/20 rule. Which 20% of work produces 80% of result?

Start 'Idea Dump' book for genius ideas you can't work on now.

Routinize your diet.

Eat healthy food.

Get delivery to save time.

Learn to ignore. No need to respond to everything.

1anage xiety~ n, swim, ince.

Do easiest things first.

1

Prioritize one item per day.

Negotiate a daily deal with your trusted cafe.

ep more. will get e done.

Do a bad first draft. You can't edit a blank page.

ag.

Set a daily routine.

No meetings unless they are decisive.

Treat time as your money.

visualized by Anna Vital

Take naps when energy runs low.

Better done than perfect.

adioma

Change your view on productivity

I could read a hundred blog posts on how
to be more productive and still find ways
to procrastinate, but these productivity
visuals (Twitter thread by @elliottaleksndr)
anchor themselves in my brain and inspire me to
reframe whatever is blocking me. This one is my favorite:

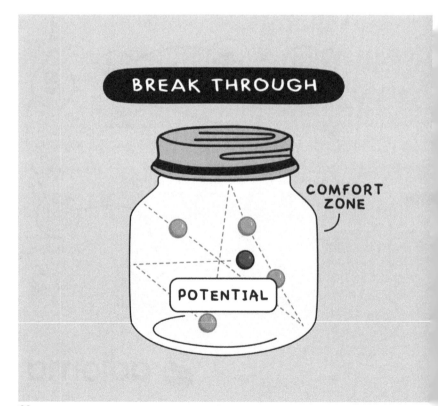

Productivity tip

Lately, I've been marking each task on my to-do list as a high-attention task or a low-attention task, and through out the day, I will alternate and work only on the things that match my energy level. I've noticed that these "energy audits" have enabled me to power through bunches of tasks that I tend to avoid because they seem tedious or time-consuming.

"To realize your existence, do the things you know you should do — the duties that echo from deep below. Stop avoiding your life."

— u/TheEmployedMoth1 on Reddit

Free printable motivational poster

This is not like those cheesy, motivational posters you've seen. This is a collection of effective action plans to defeat procrastination by Alex Vermeer. Every tip feels new and helpful and mind-opening. You can download your own poster to print out here.

How to Get Motivated

A Guide for Defeating Procrastination

Increase Value	Find Passion	Mix Bitter & Sweet	Add Accountability	Use Productive Procrastination	Keep Your Brain Healthy	Create a Reward	Get Some Energy	Create Competition	Find Flow	Find Meaning		Get Motivated
												Start
												What are you avoiding?
								Turn it into a game, make it fun!				What are you not motivated to do?
						Make the situation more rewarding.		Compete against others		How does this connect?		Be Specific!
		Combine long-term interests with short-term gains.		What can you avoid doing by doing this?		Reward your success.		Compete against yourself.		Set and review your major life goals.		
Increase Value	Find Passion	Mix Bitter & Sweet	Add Accountability	Use Productive Procrastination	Keep Your Brain Healthy	Create a Reward	Get Some Energy	Create Competition	Find Flow	Find Meaning		**Get Motivated**
	Know what you are passionate about.		Who knows about this?		Get enough sleep.		Get your blood moving.		Match difficulty with skill.			
	Is this connected?		Can you make it public?		Exercise regularly.		Splash cold water on your face.		Too easy? Make it harder. Too hard? Make it easier.		Remember: lack of effort guarantees failure!	Action is Required
	Is this intrinsically motivating?				Take genuine breaks.		Eat well.					Recognize Success
					Reduce your commitments.		Energise your environment. (e.g. music)		Make your inspirations visible.	Know what inspires you and why.	Review your inspirations.	Get Inspired
							Plan around your energy, not time.					Plan for the Worst, Hope for the Best
									Remember that you are human.	Log your procrastination habits.	Don't trivialise "I'll only give in once."	Accept Your Procrastination
												Contrast
										Nothing is carved in stone.	Qualities and skills are cultivated through effort.	Check Your Mindset
												Increase Expectancy

The Procrastination Equation

The Procrastination Equation—discussed in detail by Piers Steel in his book by the same name—accounts for every major scientific finding on procrastination and draws upon the best current theories of motivation. It looks like this:

$$Motivation = \frac{Expectancy \times Value}{Impulsiveness \times Delay}$$

Expectancy refers to the perceived odds of getting a reward and whether we expect success or failure.

Value refers to the pleasantness of doing a task, and the size of its reward.

Impulsiveness refers to the tendency to get distracted or lose focus on a task.

Delay refers to the time between the present and a task's reward or completion.

How to Get Motivated

The solution is simple. To increase motivation and decrease procrastination you must:

▲ Increase our **Expectancy** of success and the certainty of being rewarded.

▲ Increase the **Value** and pleasantness of doing a task.

▽ Decrease our **Impulsiveness** by removing distractions and maintaining focus.

▼ Decrease the **Delay** of the reward by having more immediate, salient deadlines.

Start

What are you avoiding?

"Achieve this" is better than "Avoid that."

What are you not motivated to do?

Input—"For x minutes."—is often better than output—"Finish this."

Focus on the abstract aspects of your temptation (not the fun parts).

Make your goals visible.

Be Specific!

Break it down!

Eliminate it! (Or hide it.)

Eliminate it! (Or hide it.)

Look at your goals.

Make them: Specific Realistic Meaningful

Recognize what is tempting you.

Recognize what is distracting you.

Read an inspiring quote.

Track your progress.

Get Motivated

| Set a Goal | Run a "Dash" | Eliminate Temptations | Make Failure Painful | Eliminate Distractions | Create Routines & Habits | Use Goal Reminders | Stop Suppressing Thoughts | Make Progress Visual | Use Negative Pairing | **Decrease Impulsiveness** |

Commit to doing it for only 5 minutes, set a timer.

How will failure be painful?

Can part of this be turned into a habit?

Do not 'force' distractions out of your head.

Pair temptations with undesirable images.

Action is Required

Make it more painful.

Can part of this be added to an existing routine?

Imagine a disastrous outcome.

Recognize Success

Achieve one goal after another.

Recognize small improvements as victories.

Keep a daily log.

Make a costly bet with someone.

Separate work and play.

Get Inspired

Schedule leisure before work.

Plan for the Worst, Hope for the Best

What could go wrong?

Draw on past experiences.

Make a backup plan.

Accept Your Procrastination

Contrast

Compare ideal state with current state.

Visualize and contrast the present and future.

Check Your Mindset

Increase Expectancy

Tips

Tip! If you feel overwhelmed by how many possible actions there are, focus on implementing *just one.*

Tip! Keep track of what works best for you.

Tip! Delay is hard to address directly. It is covered in other actions, especially Set a Goal under Decrease Impulsiveness.

Tip! If you run into problems, always remember the main reason for the action: to either increase value, increase expectancy, decrease impulsiveness, or decrease delay.

Acknowledgements

This poster was inspired by *The Procrastination Equation* by Piers Steel. See this book for extensive detail on the causes of procrastination and the many methods for defeating it. Buy his book and support the scientific investigation of procrastination and motivation!

How to Get Motivated v2.0 by Alex Vermeer

Also check out:
alexvermeer.com/getmotivated

How to Use This Poster

1. Notice when you are procrastinating. Be specific about what you are avoiding.

2. Pick an action from one of the three branches to either increase value, increase expectancy, or decrease impulsiveness.

3. Use the tips to help you implement the action.

4. Repeat Steps 1-3 until you are motivated.

Work from home successfully

I work from home four days a week and what helps me be most productive is having a separate work space (not in a bedroom) with lots of natural light, getting dressed as if I'm going to the office, sticking to a 9-5 schedule, and giving myself short breaks every hour to walk around or cuddle with my dog. Eating lunch away from my desk is something I have to get better at, and one thing I hadn't considered is to do some work before breakfast:

"The usual recommendation is to start with a healthy breakfast, to fuel you for your busy day ahead. However, when you're home all day, breakfast can be a drawn-out luxury, with reading, checking social media, and other distractions preventing you from getting started. Try diving into a quick work task, checking it off the list, and then sitting down to breakfast."

This article on How to Work From Home and Actually Get Stuff Done has a lot more suggestions for successfully working from home.

Ergonomic Wireless Mouse

My Magic Mouse was giving me claw hand
from the way I had to grip it and I needed to
a find an alternative mouse, so I immediately
googled Wirecutter's tested picks and bought
their upgrade pick of the Logitech MX Master
Mouse. My favorite thing about this mouse is I was able to
customize the buttons and scroll wheels to do everything my
Magic Mouse used to do.

Best lap desk

One thing that has been making my workday
easy and versatile is this very comfortable, useful
lap desk by LapGear. On it, I can fit my 17"
Macbook, my mouse, and my phone. Which
means I can easily switch up my workspace by
moving it to my recliner or couch and still be productive.

Work boundaries

"'No.' is a complete sentence."

— Unknown

Find out if you're close to burnout

IT Burnout Index is a 10-question survey that will
tell you how close you are to burnout, and what
your risk level is for Exhaustion, Self Inefficacy,
Cynicism and Depersonalization. It only takes
2 minutes to get the results and you can then
choose to check out Yerbo's personalized insights and exercises.
It's anonymous, and doesn't require an email.

How to set boundaries with your to-do list

When writing out my daily to-do list I often remember this
advice tweeted by Writer Jenée Desmond-Harris:

"I started dividing my to-do list into 1) things I have to do, 2)
things I want to do, and 3) things other people want me to do.
Life changing! I often don't get to 3 and I finally realized omg, is
this what it means to have boundaries?!"

*"We suffer more in imagination than in
reality."*

—Seneca

A guide for daily "professional" interactions

How to Professionally Say is a list of things you might feel like saying at work and the alternative — more professional way — you should say it. Some examples are:

- Instead of saying "That sounds like a horrible idea," you can say "Are we confident that this is the best solution or are we still exploring alternatives?"
- Instead of saying "You are overcomplicating this," you can say "Being mindful of timelines. Let's concentrate on the initial scope."
- Instead of saying "Did you even read my email?" you can say "Reattaching my email to provide further clarity."
- Instead of saying "Can you answer all of the questions I asked and not just pick and choose one," you can say "Are you able to provide some clarity around the other questions previously asked?"

This guide was inspired and compiled from content created by @loewhaley on Instagram, and while some of it might not flow comfortably out of my mouth, I'm inspired to adopt more neutrality and directness in my professional language.

Alternatives for "Sorry for my delay"

I feel like a weight has been lifted after reading What if we just stopped being so available? Joe Pinsker rants about the expectations of prompt responses and how we should all stop apologizing for failing to meet them.

He says, *"For one thing, having multiple obligations and priorities means that we are, all of us, in a perpetual state of delay on something, and apologizing for that fact feels like having to apologize for your standard mode of being."*

He spoke with communication experts who suggest alternatives for "Sorry for my delay," like "Thank you for your patience" or "I wanted to make sure I thought carefully about your good questions." But I agree with Pinsker who prefers to omit an apology or expectation altogether and instead just write your message as if you're responding right away, because content is more important than speed.

This article is a much needed absolution. We all have the right to disconnect.

Templates for saying no

How to say no is a collection of email templates that you can use to decline social events, meetings, dates, phone chats and other work-related requests you might get. Some of these are examples given by notable productivity experts like James Clear and Tim Ferris. You can even download these canned templates and install them into your gmail. Below are two examples:

How to say no to a phone call (keep things over email).
Hey {{first_name}},
Thanks so much for reaching out.
My schedule has been crazy lately, and these days, email is usually more convenient for me instead of the phone. Would you mind if we kept the discussion here?

How to say no to a project at work.
Hello [Name],
Thanks for thinking of me for [project]. However, I'm going to have to turn this down.
I want to ensure I continue to do my best with my existing workload and my plate's a little too full for me to be able to take this on right now.

Writing

"Writing is prayer."

— Franz Kafka

One sentence email tips

My work revolves around my inbox, so I really appreciate Josh Spector's collection of 40 concepts to help you write better emails and optimize your inbox. Below are some good ones.

- The more ideas you try to communicate in a single email, the more likely one will be overlooked.
- You don't need to sign your name at the end of your email—the recipient knows who it's from.
- The more your email sounds like you speak, the more effective it will be.
- If you're not working on email now, your inbox shouldn't be open now.
- The most important sentence in any email is the first one.
- No one ever says "I wish the paragraphs in that email were longer."
- Every email should tell the recipient what you want them to do after they read it.

"The only thing that isn't worthless: to live this life out truthfully and rightly. And be patient with those who don't."

— Marcus Aurelius

Compose better emails

I've gotten too casual with my email correspondence and this blog post on "How to write better emails" by Lazarus Lazaridis reminded me that I should strive to be more effective and efficient with my communication.
All of the tips are useful but the ones I really need to work on are:

- Use specific dates instead of "yesterday" or "tomorrow."
- Use links for references to save the reader time and eliminate ambiguity.
- Be specific on what you request from whom by referring to each recipient explicitly using the @ symbol.

Personal letter writing tips

These tips from Hallmark Card writer Courtney Faye Taylor on letter writing reminded me of all the things to keep in mind when penning a message, like leading with vulnerability and curiosity. She suggests not just sharing facts about your life, but the feelings behind them, because when you give someone a window into your personal experience you're also creating a space for them to do the same.

How to ask useful questions

This is a great blog post on "How to Ask Useful Questions," by Josh Kaufman. Poorly worded questions don't respect the recipient's time, energy or attention, and as a result often go unanswered.

An inexperienced question might sound like "I'm thinking about [action]. What do you think?" If your intention was to ask for help, a better worded question would be: "I'm trying to A, and I'm having trouble. So far, I've tried B with result C, and D with result E. Now I'm stuck. Any guidance?"

Josh gives a few more examples based on what your intention is, like asking for agreement, information, clarification, etc. The goal is to be specific, and give as much context as possible in a concise way. And of course, be polite.

Write 5x more but write 5x less

Mike Crittenden says there are 2 things he has come to believe about writing: 1. The average person should write 5x more things than they do. 2. The average written thing should be 5x shorter than it is. I remind myself of this every time I'm about to put my pen down or stop typing.

Crowdsourced writing advice

Someone asked on Reddit recently "What is the piece of writing advice that has helped you most, personally?" and these were my favorite because I had never heard them before:

- "Make the familiar seem exotic and the exotic seem familiar."
- On process, Chuck Wendig: "The work doesn't need your confidence. The work just needs the work."
- "It's easier to write something cool and then figure out how it makes sense than it is to write something that makes sense and then figure out how to make it cool."

I didn't contribute to the thread, but if I would have I would have shared Derek Sivers' genius advice: Write one sentence per line.

Proofreading hack

Sometimes my eyes deceive me when proofreading. My trick for proofing long paragraphs is to right click on them and then select Speech > Start Speaking. If it sounds off, it usually means I dropped a word.

Community-driven thesaurus

I keep PowerThesaurus.org bookmarked in my toolbar. It's the fastest way to find the word I want to use.

Search for example sentences

If I'm not confident with how I've used an expression, I will google the turn of phrase inside of quotation marks, and if I get Google Books results with similar examples then I know I've used it correctly. Lately, I've been using Ludwig. guru for the same kind of phrase searches. I like that it gives me back example sentences from different sources like encyclopedias, news and science publications.

Q&A site for all your English questions

When I can't find the right word or phrasing using Power Thesaurus or Ludwig, I'm on the English StackExchange searching for answers or posting questions. You can ask anything relating to grammar or usage or word choice and English experts will start responding right away.

Style guide for sensitive words

Language evolves fast and it's easy to slip up and say the wrong thing. Language, please is an up-to-date resource for writers navigating sensitive subjects like trauma, substance use, race, disabilities, gender, etc. I searched for the word "homeless" and I agree that "people without housing," or a "person experiencing homelessness" is a lot less stigmatizing and a better term to use.

A website of untranslatable words

I enjoy browsing Eunoia.world, a website of words that don't translate, and I'm intrigued by the concepts I had no idea existed, like "qarrtsiluni," a North Alaskan Inupiatun word for sitting in the darkness, waiting for inspiration to strike you, or " razbliuto," a Russian word to describe the feeling for someone you used to love but no longer do, or "vellichor," which I think may be made up but is a much needed word to address "the strange wistfulness of used bookstores." It's weird how once I learn a word for something I was not aware of before that I can instantly recall feeling it in the past. I would like to know the word for that.

"Advice? I don't have advice. Stop aspiring and start writing. If you're writing, you're a writer. Write like you're a goddamn death row inmate and the governor is out of the country and there's no chance for a pardon. Write like you're clinging to the edge of a cliff, white knuckles, on your last breath, and you've got just one last thing to say, like you're a bird flying over us and you can see everything, and please, for God's sake, tell us something that will save us from ourselves. Take a deep breath and tell us your deepest, darkest secret, so we can wipe our brow and know that we're not alone. Write like you have a message from the king. Or don't. Who knows, maybe you're one of the lucky ones who doesn't have to."

— Alan Watts

Index

Index

Made in the USA
Monee, IL
16 December 2022